PRIVATE EYE

Colemanballs
8

A selection of quotes,
most of which originally appeared
in PRIVATE EYE's
'Colemanballs' column.

Our thanks once again to all the readers
who sent us their contributions,
and to whom this book is dedicated.

COLEMANBALLS TOP TEN

PLACE	NAME	ENTRIES
1	DAVID COLEMAN	106
2	MURRAY WALKER	73
3	SIMON BATES	51
4	TED LOWE	37
5	HARRY CARPENTER	22
6	JOHN MOTSON	22
7	BRIAN MOORE	21
8	BRYON BUTLER	15
9	BOBBY ROBSON	15
10	TREVOR BAILEY	14
11	RON ATKINSON	14
12	FRANK BRUNO	14
13	ELTON WELSBY	9
14	GEOFFREY BOYCOTT	8

COMPOSITE TOTAL FIGURES COMPILED BY THE NEASDEN INSTITUTE OF STATISTICS, E&OE

PRIVATE EYE

Colemanballs

8

Compiled and edited by
BARRY FANTONI

Illustrated by Larry

PRIVATE EYE • CORGI

Published in Great Britain
by Private Eye Productions Ltd,
6 Carlisle Street, London W1V 5RG,
in association with Corgi Books

©1996 Pressdram Ltd
ISBN 0 552 14521 1
Designed by Bridget Tisdall
Printed in Great Britain by
Cox and Wyman Ltd, Reading

Corgi Books are published by Transworld Publishers Ltd,
61-63 Uxbridge Road, Ealing, London W5 5SA,
in Australia by Transworld Publishers (Australia) Pty, Ltd,
15-23 Helles Avenue, Moorebank, NSW 2170
and in New Zealand by Transworld Publishers (N.Z.) Ltd,
Cnr. Moselle and Waipareira Avenues, Henderson, Auckland

2 4 6 8 10 9 7 5 3 1

Athletics

"She's letting her legs do the running…"
BRENDAN FOSTER

"He seems to have had a problem with his right foot which has run with him all day."
ROBIN JACKMAN

"He's seven seconds ahead and that's a good question…"
DAVID COLEMAN

"It's your peripheral vision that goes when you're really exhausted — it's impossible to see anything directly in front of you."

SALLY GUNNELL

"Nobody has ever won the title twice before. He [Roger Black] has already done that."

DAVID COLEMAN

"I think, there is no doubt, she'll probably qualify for the final."

DAVID COLEMAN

"The reason he [Pinto] is so far ahead is because he's going so quickly."

CHARLIE SPEDDING

"This evening is a very different evening from the morning that we had this morning."

DAVID COLEMAN

"Once he'd gone past the point of no return, there was no going back."

COMMENTATOR, BBC1

"…and Ottey, still running supremely well, takes the silver."

DAVID COLEMAN

"Mixed fortunes favour the brave…"

DAVID COLEMAN

"Christie… clearly has hamstring trouble — we think."

DAVID COLEMAN

"I have the feeling she [Manuela Machado] is an athlete who likes to get away from the opposition."

DAVID COLEMAN

Boxing

"I stand a 50-50 chance, if not 60-50, against anyone out there."

FRANK BRUNO

"I've had 38 fights, lost one and was never put on my feet."

GARY MASON

"I think it was the clash of styles that made it a good fight; we both have similar styles."

LENNOX LEWIS

"He [Mike Tyson] will have to go into a room by himself and get used to seeing the outside world again."

FRANK BRUNO

"I truly believe that the confidence I have is unbelievable."

PRINCE NAZEEM HAMED

Classic FM

"…and now, from the World of the Bartered Bride to the World of Opera…"

SUSANNAH SIMONS

"Beethoven… interesting to hear his Symphony No.1. Obviously his very first symphony."

NICK BAILEY

"Beautifully played, as ever, by a man celebrating his birthday this year…"

HENRY KELLY

"And that was the second movement of Beethoven's 7th Symphony by… er…Beethoven."

PRESENTER

Cricket

"I presented my trousers to the committee: I had nothing to hide."

MIKE ATHERTON

"You can't get any earlier than the second ball of the game."

DAVID LLOYD

"You've got to make split-second decisions so quickly."

GEOFFREY BOYCOTT

"The only person who could be better than Brian Lara, could be Brian Lara himself."

COLIN CROFT

"Jack Russell may be the artist, but Metson showed he's a rhyming couplet of a wicketkeeper."

REPORTER, RADIO FIVE

"He [Courtney Walsh] ripped the heart out of England, both metaphorically and physically."

COMMENTATOR, BBC

"Nigeria... very much the dark horses of this tournament."

ROB BAILEY

"It was all so easy for Walsh. All he had to do was drop an arm and there it was, on the ground!"

TONY LEWIS

"And the rest not only is history but will remain history for many years to come."

JACK BANNISTER

"Everything in Halifax's favour is against them tonight."

EDDIE HEMMINGS

"Mike Atherton's a thinking captain… he gives the impression of someone with his head on all the time."

COLIN CROFT

"This run of 24 games without defeat… must be like a millstone on your shoulders."

TONY GUBBA

"Now Ramprakash is facing a fish of a rather different feather in Mark Waugh."

PETER BAXTER

"Glen McGrath bowled so badly in his first Test, as though he'd never bowled in a Test Match before."

GEOFFREY BOYCOTT

"Sean Pollock there, a carbon copy of his dad.
Except he's a bit taller and he's got red hair."

TREVOR BAILEY

"England might now be the favourites to draw this
match."

VIC MARKS

"[Gavin Larsen] is inexperienced in Test Cricket,
in that this is his first Test."

GEOFFREY BOYCOTT

"And this game is coming nicely to a climax…
like a well-cooked Welsh rabbit."

COMMENTATOR, RADIO 4

"Michael Atherton must think all his Christmases
are coming home at once

GEOFFREY BOYCOTT

"Fortunately it was a slow ball — so it wasn't a fast one."

GEOFFREY BOYCOTT

"…nearly 34 — in fact he's 33."

RICHIE BENAUD

Darts

"Under that heart of stone beat muscles of pure flint."

SID WADDELL

Football

"He's one of those managers you'd give your left leg to play for."

COLIN COOPER

"A win would be better than a draw."

DENIS LAW

"This game is simmering… that explosion shows you just how close it could be to exploding."

ALAN PARRY

"A game is not won until it is lost."

DAVID PLEAT

"If you were in the Brondby dressing room right now, which of the Liverpool players would you be looking at?"

RAY STUBBS

"He's caused the Chelsea defence no amount of problems."

JIMMY ARMFIELD

"Ogrizovic was in two minds as to whether to go or stay and in the end he did neither."

JEFF FOSTER, CWR RADIO

"They've really got the bit between their legs now…"

BOBBY HAM

"We [England] haven't been scoring goals, but football's not just about scoring goals. It's about winning."

ALAN SHEARER

"This tall, six-footed, tanned referee from Spain…"

JOHN CHAMPION

"They didn't change positions, they just moved the players around."

TERRY VENABLES

"We deserved to win this game after hammering them 0-0 in the first half."

KEVIN KEEGAN

"Football today, it's like a game of chess. It's all about money."

NEWCASTLE UNITED FAN

"Barry Fry is a real kleptomaniac. He sees a player and then has to go and buy him."

TONY FRANCIS

"As with most things in football the goalposts keep changing."

DAVID RHODES

"He [Brian Laudrup] wasn't just facing one defender — he was facing one at the front and one at the back as well."

TREVOR STEVEN

"His goal famine was like manna from heaven."

KEVIN KEEGAN

"Amin [of Saudi Arabia] has passed the ball more like Idi Amin. And even he'd struggle in this heat, big Idi…"

COMMENTATOR, ITV

"Yes, six inches either side of the post and that would have been a goal…"

COMMENTATOR, RADIO NEWCASTLE

"They already know who they'll be playing in the semi-final — the winner of the Nantes v Spartak Moscow game."

ALAN PARRY

"The lad got over-excited when he saw the whites of the goalpost's eyes."

STEVE COPPELL

"The new West Stand casts a giant shadow over the entire pitch, even on a sunny day."

CHRIS JONES

"What will you do when you leave football, Jack — will you stay in football?"

STUART HALL

"If you closed your eyes you would think it was Maradona."

BOB WILSON

"Ruud Gullit was able to impose his multi-lingual skills on this match."

JOHN MOTSON

"If you want change, you've got to stick with it."
TERRY VENABLES

"You sometimes open your mouth and it punches you straight between the eyes…"

PADDY CRERAND

"And I suppose they [Spurs] are nearer to being out of the FA Cup now than any other time since the first half of this season, when they weren't ever in it anyway."

JOHN MOTSON

"When you're down, you Palace fans, the fickle finger of fate rarely smiles on you."

JONATHAN PEARCE

"Ally McCoist will always get you a goal, whether he's playing or on the bench."

MARK HATELEY

"He's one of those footballers whose brains are in his head…"

DEREK JOHNSTONE

"What disappointed me was that we didn't play with any passion. I'm not disappointed, you know, I'm just disappointed."

KEVIN KEEGAN

"It's now 1-1, an exact reversal of the score on Saturday."

COMMENTATOR, RADIO 5 LIVE

"I've lost count of how many corners there have been. Lincoln have had 1, and Crystal Palace 17."

RON JONES

"The tackles are coming in thick and thin now."

ALAN BRAZIL

"He's carrying his left leg, which, to be honest, is his only leg…"

STEVE COPPELL

"The lads really ran their socks into the ground."
ALEX FERGUSON

"...and the steam has gone completely out of the Spanish sails..."

DAVID PLEAT

"The game was continuous for the whole of the first forty-five minutes."

JACK CHARLTON

"That was a big relief off me shoulder…"

PAUL GASCOIGNE

"It's a lot harder to play football when you haven't got the ball."

ANDY GRAY

"…not one Millwall player surrounded the referee there."

DAVID PLEAT

"Stoichkov's had a quiet game, but that's often the hallmark of greatness."

MIKE INGHAM

"Julian Dicks is everywhere. It's like they've got eleven Dicks on the field."

COMMENTATOR, METRO RADIO

"We say 'educated left foot' — of course, there are many players with educated right foots."

RON JONES

"That's twice now he [Terry Phelan] has got between himself and the goal."

BRIAN MARWOOD

"Gary [Cole] always weighed up his options, especially when he had no choice."

KEVIN KEEGAN

"He may yet pull this team from the edge of the cliff by the scruff of its neck into the land of milk and honey."

JONATHAN HAYWARD

"Raith Rovers have never won a major trophy during their distinguished career."

RAY STUBBS

"For all the money in China, you think Francis is going to get that ball."

RON ATKINSON

"And don't forget tomorrow night — the whole of Newcastle versus Manchester United."

COMMENTATOR, RADIO 5

"They [Swindon] are still finding that they are much happier when they have the ball than when the other side has it."

RON JONES

"You can tell by his body language that his head's on the floor."

RAY WILKINS

"Players prefer the FA Cup because it's the end of season curtain-raiser."

PETER WITHE

"We want a game where the players are beyond repute."

ALAN SMITHSON

"They're still in the game and they're trying to get back into it."

JIMMY HILL

"This is the worst day for Newcastle since Custer's last stand against the Sioux."

ALAN MULLERY

"...and some 500 Italians made the trip, in a crowd of only 400."

DAVID SMITH

"If it stays as it is I can't see it altering."

GRAHAM TAYLOR

"...you look at the West Bromwich players and you get the feeling their heads have wilted..."

RON ATKINSON

"If you can lipread, you'll be able to tell from his arm signals that it's broken."

TREVOR FRANCIS

"Castleford are looking down the barrel of a far different match."

MAURICE BAMFORD

"…and he crosses the line with the ball almost mesmerically tied to his foot with a ball of string…"

IAN DARKE

"I would place him [FC Porto goalkeeper] as the number one in Europe, if you really put me on the fence."

BOBBY ROBSON

"They [Rosenborg] have won 66 games, and they've scored in all of them."

BRIAN MOORE

"Diego Maradona — a flawed genius who has now become a genius who is flawed."

BOB WILSON

"Unfortunately, we keep kicking ourselves in the foot."

RAY WILKINS

"Actually, none of the players are wearing earrings; Kjeldberg, with his contact lenses, is the closest we can get."

JOHN MOTSON

"Every single seat is absolutely packed."

RON JONES

"The referees had a generally good game and only put a few feet wrong

RAY WILKINS

"Steve McMahon... born in the shadow of the Mersey..."

ALAN PARRY

"The fallout from the World Cup saw a galaxy of stars land on Planet Premiership."

JOHN MOTSON

"We threw our dice into the ring and turned up trumps."

BRUCE RIOCH

"Hoddle by name, Hoddle by nature…"

COMMENTATOR, BBC1

"They've made a good start. Now it's my job to get their heads back on the ground."

BILLY AYRES

"His talent was teeming out of his ears when he had the ball at his feet."

BRIAN CLOUGH

"The United forward line, like professional undertakers, are now dancing on the graves of their opponent's defence."

COMMENTATOR, RADIO LANCASHIRE

"Give him his head and he'll take it with both feet or hands."

BOBBY GOULD

"Henning Berg…one of the players classified as a foreigner — which obviously as a Norwegian is something he's used to…"

GUY HABBORD

Golf

"That was a beautiful shot. Inch perfect – but an inch wide."

COMMENTATOR, BBC2

Horse Racing

"The racecourse is as level as a billiard ball."

JOHN FRANCOME, CHANNEL 4

"There is a lot of water under the bridge yet to come."

JIMMY LINDLEY

Ice Hockey

"Three-nothing Finland. And Russia are lucky to get nothing."

ICE-HOCKEY COMMENTATOR, BBC2

Literally

"Sammy Cahn literally put the words into Frank Sinatra's mouth."

ITN

"The Labour Party survey says that dentists have literally been kicked in the teeth."

NEIL DIXON

"So astronomers were excited by the discovery of a major new spiral galaxy Dwingeloo 1 – literally on Earth's doorstep."

NEW SCIENTIST

"Sid [Field] used to come on stage and literally open his heart out to the audience."

DAVID SUCHET

"Many pilots shot down in the war, were literally guinea pigs."

BBC SOUTH

"At half time Ardiles said go out there and throw the kitchen sink at them. Spurs are doing that… literally."

ALAN MULLERY

"The ball came back, literally cutting him [Graham Thorpe] in half."

COLIN CROFT

"When they go into mass-production the prices will come tumbling down, literally like peas in a pod."

TECHNO-GURU, RADIO FIVE LIVE

"The Royal Family could literally be sitting on a gold mine, if the search for oil beneath Windsor Castle proves successful."

LONDON TONIGHT

"Paul Harkin literally kicked Wigan to death in the semi-final last week."

RAY FRENCH

"Mr Portillo has opened up literally a can of spending worms."

MICHAEL BRUNSON

"The Embassy final has literally turned into a Greek Tragedy for Alan Warriner."

SID WADDELL

"This is the sort of pitch which literally castrates a bowler."

TREVOR BAILEY

"The flavour is out of this world. I mean that literally."

DELIA SMITH

"Nethercott, literally standing in Le Tissier's pocket…"

DAVID PLEAT

"We're talking to Frank Bruno this morning and the phones have literally been melting."

'MOTORMOUTH' PRESENTER, ITV

"Tonight, literally getting off his deathbed — Elvis Costello…"

DANNY BAKER

"She went off so fast she literally died in the last 50 metres."

SALLY GUNNELL

"We now go to Gibraltar to talk to Carmen Proetta, who was literally torn to pieces by the British press."

DAVID DUNSEITH

"Following the announcement, the soldiers are literally glued to their radios."

STEVEN SACKER

Mastermind

"If I get more questions right than anyone else I think I will win."

MELVYN KINSEY

Motor Sport

"…and Mark Blundell stops with his front wheels stationary."

MURRAY WALKER

"This is lap 54 — after that it's 55, 56, 57, 58…"

MURRAY WALKER

"Well, we now have exactly the same situation as at the beginning of the race, only exactly opposite."

MURRAY WALKER

"The faster he goes the quicker he'll get to the pits — the slower he goes the longer it will take."

MURRAY WALKER

"Schumacher… he is either coming into the pits on this lap or he is not…"

MURRAY WALKER

"So that's 24 points for Schumacher and 23 points for Hill — so there's only one point between them if my mental arithmetic is correct."

MURRAY WALKER

"And now, excuse me while I interrupt myself."

MURRAY WALKER

"Ericsson's record is second to none in the RAC Rally — he's been second three times."

MITSUBISHI MOTORS SPOKESMAN

"Schumacher, virtually pedalling his Benetton back with his fists."

MURRAY WALKER

"Veteran BBC commentator Murray Walker said it was the blackest day for Grand Prix racing since he had started covering the sport."

BBC TELETEXT NEWS (AFTER THE DEATH OF AYRTON SENNA)

"He [Katayama] can't decide whether to have his visor half open or half closed."

MURRAY WALKER

"And on lap 72 out of 71, Damon Hill leads…"

MURRAY WALKER

"Even in five years' time, he [David Coulthard] will still be four years younger than Damon Hill."

JONATHAN PALMERN

"It looks as though this year there will be seventeen Grand Prix for the World Championship, compared with the traditional seventeen."

MURRAY WALKER

Oddballs

"And for the rest of Europe this weekend, a lot of cloud around in the form of cloud..."

SUZANNE CHARLTON

"Jersey's Crime Prevention Team are out and about, so have you locked up your property?"
ROGER BARA

"I'm a bit of a technophobe – I love technology."
STEVE ALLEN

"The original light bulb invented by Thomas Edison goes under the hammer at Sothebys today"
COMMENTATOR, LONDON NEWS RADIO

"They have opened a Pandora's box of worms."
                                    MICHAEL WHITE

"Because of demand, we will be seeking to
reintroduce non-stop flights across the Atlantic."
                                    FREDDIE LAKER

"For most people, death comes at the end of their
lives."
                                    EXPERT, GLR

"That was no bed of cherries…"
                                    MARK STEIN

"The young aren't interested in mime nowadays. It has nothing to say to them."

EXPERT, RADIO 4

"If you're frightened of the fat, then stay out of the fire…"

ALASTAIR MACAULEY

"In Japan, I suppose, apples are small bananas compared to rice."

RHOD SHARPVINE

"Red squirrels… you don't see many of them since they became extinct."

MICHAEL ASPEL

"It has been one of the warmest 1994s this century."

RICHARD ALLINSON

"The men have been transferred to Bracknell police station — which has been the scene of police activity all day."

NEWSREADER, BBC1

"So you both work in Intensive Care. Any funny stories there?"

TIM VINE

"The attack appears to be absolutely randomless."

ALAN ROBB

"So that cloud's moving away and the rain is clearing up, so that's good news for the Netherlands and it's good news for Holland as well."

WEATHER FORECASTER, GMTV

"The difference between Page 3 and men's magazines is a big yawning chasm…"

TRACEY ELVICK

"The old warhorse once again has pulled a hat out of the bag."

NICK ROSS

"Thanks very much for your thought provoking thoughts which were very thought provoking."

DAVID FROST

"I watched that without the sound, so I couldn't quite see what was going on."

ADRIAN CHILDS

"…with a few hiccups people can overcome it [alcoholism]."

SPOKESMAN FOR ALCOHOL CONCERN

"Christmas is far too commercial, and toilet paper with Father Christmas on it is scraping the bottom…"

EXPERT, RADIO 4

"The Indian meal is firmly embedded in the English conscience."

LLOYD GROSSMAN

"We've heard these arguments about drift nets before, and they just don't hold water."

FISHERMEN'S SPOKESMAN, RADIO 4

"Fifteen per cent of people with serious mental illness commit suicide during their lifetime."

CHRIS BORN, BATH MENTAL HEALTH UNIT, BBC

"It's not so much a thankless task, it's more a job with no thanks."

COLIN BAKER

"50% of the women going into the profession [law] are now women."

JANE WHITTAKER

"As a mark of respect to the RAF airmen who were killed yesterday, we will not be showing 'Best of Biggin Hill' as advertised. Instead, here's 'Highway to Heaven'."

ANNOUNCER, MERIDIAN TV

"All our trains were fully booked, and that's what caused the problem."

EUROTUNNEL SPOKESMAN

"The clock is going to tick one way or the other."

JIM NAUGHTIE

"People in Italy are not having enough babies, and the population is in decline. Those in the south are keeping their end up, but cannot make up for the decline in the north."

EXPERT, TV EURONEWS

"I employed Alistair Campbell *and* Charles Lewington. I suppose that makes a hat-trick."

EVE POLLARD

"A great shadow has been lifted from my shoulders."

PC GUSCOTT

Politics

"Mr Lewis has been head of the Prison Service for two years and during that time a great deal of progress has been made, particularly in terms of escapes."

MICHAEL HOWARD

"It's not the future I'm talking about, I'm talking about tomorrow…"

JOHN GUMMER

"If Europe stays still it will start going backwards."

PADDY ASHDOWN

"…this white paper is a waste of the money it's printed on."

MATHEW TAYLOR

"If you won't tell me who told you that, it's not worth the paper it's written on."

MALCOLM RIFKIND

"The IRA have been isolated in the eyes of the world and many other people."

JOHN MAJOR

"I think that ministers over the years have not seen this problem coming, because it has been coming for a long time."

NICHOLAS SOAMES

"Anyone would think we were living on some island somewhere."

GEORGE WALDEN

"Anybody in my job steers a tightrope between being popular and being principled."

VIRGINIA BOTTOMLEY

"To coin a phrase, he was a phoenix with nine lives."

SIMON HEFFER

"We need to get rid of those old archaic practices which have been built up since 1990."

BOB HORTON

"It's no use trying to pin a donkey on a few individuals, however much Lord Justice Scott wants to."

ALAN CLARKE

"I know I'm treading into a mine field and I'll have to sink or swim."

ANNE SMITH

"Here we have a government disintegrating between our eyes…"

JOHN PRESCOTT

"All the Cabinet Ministers sat around the table with their heads nodding like cuckoo clocks."

ENOCH POWELL

"...and if I could just correct one fact..."

JOHN PRESCOTT

...the Secretary of State has taken the brakes off the log jam."

CHRISTINE HANCOCK

"Every syllable the Prime minister utters will be pored over, even if he doesn't say anything at all."

PETER SPENCER

"That's a fascinating crystal ball, I'll tell you the other side of that coin."

LORD ARCHER

"He [Norman Lamont] knows his political future is now behind him."

TONY BANKS

"John Redwood is a young man but, let's face it, so was Margaret Thatcher in 1975."

EDWARD LEIGH

"Jim Callaghan had a good ear for the wind blowing from the grass roots."

SHIRLEY WILLIAMS

"There is a vast degree of sleaze, more than actually exists."

ROBIN OAKLEY

"The more important things are more important than the less important."

STEPHEN DORRELL

"Two things are absolutely clear, and I want to make them absolutely clear."

HARRIET HARMAN

"Adams now wants that self-respect from other people."

EXPERT, RADIO 5

"The world has gone through tremendous change recently; both nationally and internationally…"

JOHN MAJOR

"…that the Government should be held to ransom by a lot of Flotsam and Bobtail…"

NORMAN LAMONT

"The government are shrugging their feet over this issue."

DOUG HOYLE

"I will turn directly to the Asylum Bill later."

JOHN MAJOR

"Bridge-building is a two-way street…"

JONATHAN AITKEN

"UN goodwill may be a bottomless pit but it's by no means limitless."

JOHN MAJOR

Pop

"There is certainly more in the future now than back in 1964."

ROGER DALTREY

"And that was Take That singing acoustically, with their own voices."

MARK GOODIER

"I've been up and down so many times that I feel as if I'm in a revolving door."

CHER

"Knowing John Lennon, who I didn't know, I don't think he would have gotten back together with them."

JOEY RAMONE

"One was called 'Whitey' for no reason at all. To be fair, his name was White."

HANK MARVIN

"So how does it feel to have your first ever debut Number One?"

DOCTOR FOX

"…and 30 years of longevity takes time to mature."

SIR CLIFF RICHARD

"…Detroit, or 'Motor Town' as they call it for short…"

LINDA LEWIS

"The Sex Pistols lasted just 18 months. Then Sid Vicious was dead. Mrs Thatcher took over."

WENDY AUSTIN

"Everyone will condemn with one hand but read avidly with the other eyeball."

JANE MOORE

"Jonathan Pryce is Jonathan Pryce: he's something else."

LIONEL BART

"and hey…Annie Lennox…everything she touches turns to gold – I guess that's why they call her Medusa…"

DR FOX

Question & Answer

RICHARD MADELEY: So how long have you been mulling over the decision to go?

JULIE GOODYEAR: Two years.

RICHARD MADELEY: So how long ago was that?

JULIE GOODYEAR: Two years ago…

ITV

ZOE BALL: So tell us what this is exactly…
GUEST: It's a matchstick model of Cardiff Arms Park.
ZOE BALL: Wow! That's amazing. What's it made out of?
GUEST: Er… matchsticks.

CHANNEL 4

JOHN HUMPHRIES: So, in one word, don't get rid of the Lottery, do it better!
SUE LAWLEY: That was two words.

RADIO 4

NEIL FOX: Prince was No. 1 last week and the week before. We want to know — how many weeks was he No. 1?"
LISTENER: Two.
FOX: Correct.

CAPITAL RADIO

JUSTINE WEBB: With John Redwood declaring, what do you do now? Do you stand back and say "Let the best man win?"
JEREMY HANLEY: No I don't. I'm right behind the Prime Minister.

BBC BREAKFAST NEWS

MARTYN LEWIS: Congratulations! Here is your round-the-world air ticket. What are you going to do with it?
CONTESTANT: Go round the world.

BBC2

CALLER: I'm a jumper presser.
CLIVE WARREN: What does that involve?
CALLER: Pressing jumpers

RADIO 1

CHRISTOPHER MARTIN-JENKINS: The New Zealand bowling has been better this morning.
TREVOR BAILEY: One reason is that they bowled better.

RADIO 4

ANNA WALKER: "Alan, can you give us the inside track on the Paul Ince, Arsenal, transfer speculation?"
ALAN SMITH *(ex-Arsenal footballer):* "Well I heard on the radio last night that the deal was still a possibility."
ANNA WALKER: "There you are, you heard it here first…"

SKY SPORTS

REPORTER: I am standing outside The Bicycle Shop with the owner. So tell me — what do you sell?
OWNER: Er, bicycles…

RADIO FORTH

JEREMY VINE: So your autobiography is out in paperback. What's it about?
LORD LONGFORD: Myself…

RADIO 5 LIVE

REPORTER: How important was it psychologically to get those six points out of the way?

TEDDY SHERINGHAM: Very psychological.

BBC1

GUEST: Our latest venture is a pizza vending machine.

SEAN BOLGER: A pizza vending machine, what does that do?

GUEST: Well, you put money into it and out comes a bit of pizza.

TALK RADIO UK

CLIVE WARREN: How many hours a week do you work?

CALLER: About 80.

CLIVE WARREN: That's 80 hours a week, then?

CALLER: Yes.

RADIO 1

RICHARD WHITELEY: You don't sound very Scottish.

CONTESTANT: That's because I'm from Liverpool.

CHANNEL 4

JAMES WHALE: And you write to the Yorkshire Ripper?
GUEST: We write to each other every day.
JAMES WHALE: How often do you write to him?
GUEST: Every day.

ITV

RICHARD MADELEY: So you were working in South Africa before Nelson Mandela was even heard of. What was South Africa known as then?
CALLER: South Africa.

ITV

CALLER: It's my 29th birthday today.
PRESENTER: Really? Wow! So when's the big 3-0?
CALLER: Next year.

TALK RADIO UK

JOHN INVERDALE: What do you think the score will be?
CALLER: Nil-all draw.
JOHN INVERDALE: So who'll score for Everton then?

RADIO FIVE LIVE

RAY STUBBS: You've been a lifelong supporter of Sheffield United…
SEAN BEAN: Yes.
STUBBS: So, how long have you been supporting them?
BEAN: Er… all my life.

BBC1

JONATHAN DIMBLEBY: Are you at secondary
school?
GIRL: Yes. I'm 14.
DIMBLEBY: How old are you?
GIRL: I'm 14.

RADIO 4

STEVE WHATLEY: Audrey in Rotherham, what
have you bought?
AUDREY: The battery recharger.
WHATLEY: What will you be using that for?

SKY TV

MAN: You see this house? I've lived here for 80 years, I was born in this house. I'm the oldest person in this street.
RICHARD ORFORD: How old are you then?
MAN: Er, I'm 80.

CHANNEL 4

DAVE LEE TRAVIS: Is it a part-time evening job?
CALLER: Yes.
DLT: When do you work, then?
CALLER: Evenings…

MINSTER FM

MARIELLA FROSTRUP: And our next caller is Gary from Streatham. Hello Gary — where are you from?
CALLER: Er… Streatham.

GLR

JONATHON COLEMAN: So you work for British Telecom?
CALLER: Yes.
COLEMAN: So why isn't it called Scottish Telecom up there in Glasgow?
CALLER: Because it's British.

VIRGIN 1215

QUESTIONMASTER: Name a drink made from fermented pears.
CONTESTANT: Apple juice.

LONDON TALKBACK RADIO

CONTESTANT: I like travelling abroad.
JIM BOWEN: To foreign countries?

ITV

LIBBY PURVES: Why call the firm 'Bloodaxe Books'?
NEIL ASTLEY: I chose it because it rhymes.

RADIO 4

LUKE JENNINGS: Where do you get your eggs?
M. ROUX: From a chicken.

ES MAGAZINE

CALLER: In my job as a pollution officer I get paid £8 to £10 each time I get called out at night.
SEAN BOLGER: I see. So how much do you get paid, then?
CALLER: How do you mean?
BOLGER: If you're called out during the night…

TALK RADIO UK

ROLF HARRIS (of a dog): He's jumping around like a two-year-old. How old is he?
MAN: "…Two…"

DENNIS PENNIS: Have you ever thought of writing your autobiography?
CHRIS EUBANK: On what?

Royals

"The monarchy should be a symbol of a classless society."

HOME SECRETARY

"Princess Anne's not afraid of a latrine in Africa
— she just gets in there and does the job."

COMMENTATOR, BBC1

Rugby

"The Japanese scrum half is quite small, but he is
very nippy…"

COMMENTATOR, EUROSPORT

"They've got their heads in the sand. It's a Canute
job!"

RUGBY UNION SPOKESMAN

"The ball is often a handicap in these conditions."
NIGEL STARMER-SMITH

"And the blue and white hoops of Sale will no doubt act as a red rag to the Tigers."
IAN BROWN

"…and in contrast we have the New Zealand team, littered with internationals."
COMMENTATOR, BBC1

"Well, they say there's no place like Wembley for the winners; and there certainly isn't for the runners-up."

COMMENTATOR, BBC1

"We all know that England are the best rugby team in the world and next weekend, when they play Scotland, we'll find out if they are the best in Britain."

LORD ARCHER

"We go to the four corners of the globe to bring you the best of Rugby League – Batley, Oldham, Wigan and France."

EDDIE HEMMINGS

"South Africa scored one try just before the break, and one just after the break, effectively finishing the game off, but, in between, England played some great rugby."

ROB ANDREW

"We have self-belief in each other."

GAVIN HASTINGS

Snooker

"He was used to being uncertain now he's not so sure."

JOHN VIRGO

"The harder it is, the more difficult."

COMMENTATOR, BBC2

"And this is, as they say, what happens next."

DAVID VINE

"This is where the precision has to be precise."

JOHN SPENCER

Tennis

"I wonder if the Germans have a word for 'Blitzkrieg' in their language?"

FREW MCMILLAN

"Sampras's heart must have been in his hands…"

COMMENTATOR, SKY

"Well… judging from his serves Larsson will either win this match or lose it."

COMMENTATOR, EUROSPORT

"She never loses a match. If she loses a match, it's because her opponent beats her."

PAM SHRIVER

"You always feel much better if someone endorses the call – even if they were wrong."

VIRGINIA WADE

"As Boris Becker sits there, his eyes staring out in front of him, I wonder what he's thinking? I think he's thinking 'I am Boris Becker'. At least, I hope that's what he's thinking."

JOHN BARRETT